Baby Birds

by Helen Frost

Consulting Editor: Gail Saunders-Smith, Ph.D.

Consultant: Ilze Balodis, Institute for
Field Ornithology, University of Maine at Machias

Pebble Books

an imprint of Capstone Press
Mankato, Minnesota

Pebble Books are published by Capstone Press
151 Good Counsel Drive, P.O. Box 669, Mankato, Minnesota 56002
http://www.capstone-press.com

2 3 4 5 6 7 07 06 05 04 03 02

Library of Congress Cataloging-in-Publication Data
Frost, Helen, 1949–
    Baby birds / by Helen Frost.
    p. cm.—(Birds)
    Summary: Describes the development of baby birds after they hatch, including
their feeding, growth of feathers, and first flight.
    ISBN 0-7368-0222-3 (hardcover)
    ISBN 0-7368-8193-X (paperback)
    1.Birds—Infancy—Juvenile literature. [1. Birds. Animals—Infancy.] I. Title.
II. Series: Frost, Helen, 1949– Birds.
QL676.2.F76 1999
598.139—dc21   98-31721

Note to Parents and Teachers

The Birds series supports national science standards related to the
diversity and unity of life. This book describes how altricial birds
develop, from hatching to leaving the nest. The American robin is
pictured in this book as an example of an altricial bird. The
photographs support early readers in understanding the text. The
repetition of words and phrases helps early readers learn new
words. This book also introduces early readers to subject-specific
vocabulary words, which are defined in the Words to Know section.
Early readers may need assistance to read some words and to use
the Table of Contents, Words to Know, Read More, Internet Sites,
and Index/Word List sections of the book.

Table of Contents

4

Baby birds hatch
from eggs.

Baby birds have
no feathers.

8

Baby birds open their bills.

Mother and father birds feed baby birds.

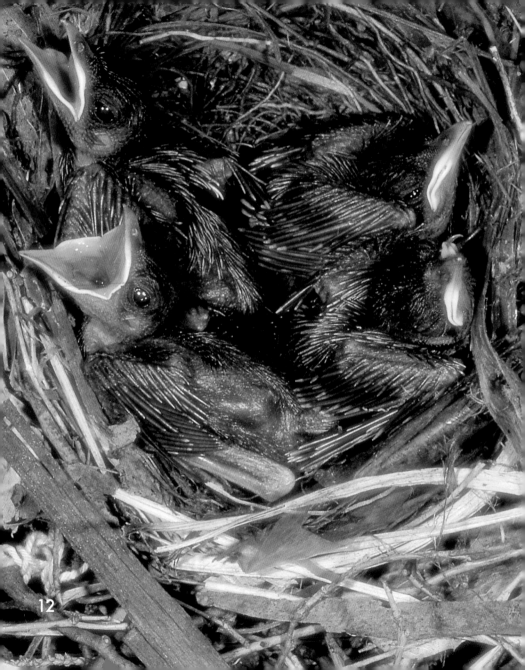

Feathers grow on the bodies of baby birds.

Feathers grow on the wings of baby birds.

Baby birds grow.

Baby birds learn
to fly.

Baby birds leave
the nest.

Words to Know

bill—the hard part of a bird's mouth; birds use their bills to eat, to carry things, and to build nests.

feathers—the light, fluffy parts of a bird that cover its body; feathers keep birds warm and help them fly.

fly—to travel through the air; baby birds learn to fly after feathers grow on their wings.

hatch—to break out of an egg

nest—a place birds build to lay their eggs and raise their young; most birds use mud, grass, plant parts, or stones to build their nests.

wings—the feather-covered limbs of a bird; birds flap their wings to help them fly.

Read More

Garcia, Eulalia. *Baby Birds: Growing and Flying.* Secrets of the Animal World. Milwaukee: Gareth Stevens, 1997.

Saunders-Smith, Gail. *Chickens.* Animals. Mankato, Minn.: Pebble Books, 1997.

Weidensaul, Scott. *National Audubon Society First Field Guide. Birds.* New York: Scholastic, 1998.

Internet Sites

All About Birds
http://www.enchantedlearning.com/subjects/birds/Allaboutbirds.html

All About Birds
http://www.iwrc-online.org/kids/Facts/Birds/bird_families.htm

Wildlife Rescue & Rehabilitation—Baby Birds
http://www.wildlife-rescue.org/birds.html

Index/Word List

Word Count: 51
Early-Intervention Level: 5

Editorial Credits

Colleen Sexton, editor; Steve Weil/Tandem Design, cover designer; Kimberly Danger and Sheri Gosewisch, photo researchers

Photo Credits

Charles W. Melton, 4
ColePhoto/Mary Clay, 6
Daybreak Imagery/Richard Day, cover
Dwight R. Kuhn, 18
Eddie Eller, 10
Joe McDonald, 16
Michael Habicht, 12
Unicorn Stock Photos/Tom Edwards, 14
Visuals Unlimited/Garry Walter, 1; D. Snyder, 8; Gary W. Carter, 20